PIRANHAS
AND OTHER SMALL DEADLY CREATURES

Tom Jackson

Crabtree Publishing Company

www.crabtreebooks.com

Crabtree Publishing Company

www.crabtreebooks.com   1-800-387-7650

Author: Tom Jackson
Project editor: Ruth Owen
Project designer: Sara Greasley
Photo research: Lizzie Knowles
Proofreaders: Crystal Sikkens
Production coordinator:
    Katherine Kantor
Prepress technicians: Ken Wright,
    Katherine Kantor

With thanks to series
editors Honor Head
and Jean Coppendale,
and consultant
Sally Morgan.

Thank you to
Lorraine Petersen
and the members
of nasen

**Published
in Canada
Crabtree Publishing**
616 Welland Ave.
St. Catharines, ON
L2M 5V6

**Published in the
United States
Crabtree Publishing**
PMB16A
350 Fifth Ave., Suite 3308
New York, NY 10118

Content development by Shakespeare Squared
www.ShakespeareSquared.com
First published in Great Britain in 2008 by ticktock Media Ltd,
2 Orchard Business Centre, North Farm Road,
Tunbridge Wells, Kent, TN2 3XF
Copyright © ticktock Entertainment Ltd 2008

Picture credits:
Corbis: Jeffrey L. Rohman: p. 17
FLPA: Mark Moffett/Minden Pictures: p. 21, 22-23; Panda
    Photo: p. 6–7; Birgitte Wilms/Minden Pictures: p. 16
Istockphoto: p. 1, 18
Nature Picture Library: Jurgen Freund: p. 8
NHPA: A.N.T. Photo Library: p. 24
Rex Features: Esther Beaton: p. 27; John Chapple: p. 26
Science Photo Library: Martin Dohrn: p. 5; Volker Steger: p. 25
Shutterstock: cover, p. 2–3, 4, 7 (inset), 9, 10–11, 12, 13,
    14–15, 15 (top inset) 19 (top), 19 (bottom), 28-29, 31

Every effort has been made to trace copyright holders, and we apologize in
advance for any omissions. We would be pleased to insert the appropriate
acknowledgments in any subsequent edition of this publication.

Library and Archives Canada Cataloguing in Publication

Jackson, Tom, 1972-
    Piranhas and other small deadly creatures / Tom Jackson.

(Crabtree contact)
Includes index.
ISBN 978-0-7787-3770-4 (bound).--ISBN 978-0-7787-3792-6 (pbk.)

    1. Dangerous animals--Juvenile literature. 2. Poisonous
animals--Juvenile literature. I. Title. II. Series.

QL100.J32 2008   j591.6'5   C2008-905958-1

Library of Congress Cataloging-in-Publication Data

Jackson, Tom, 1972-
    Piranhas and other small deadly creatures / Tom Jackson.
        p. cm. -- (Crabtree contact)
Includes index.
    ISBN-13: 978-0-7787-3792-6 (pbk. : alk. paper)
    ISBN-10: 0-7787-3792-6 (pbk. : alk. paper)
    ISBN-13: 978-0-7787-3770-4 (reinforced library binding : alk. paper)
    ISBN-10: 0-7787-3770-5 (reinforced library binding : alk. paper)
    1. Dangerous animals--Juvenile literature. 2. Poisonous animals--
Juvenile literature. I. Title. II. Series.

QL100.J33 2009
591.6'5--dc22

        2008039405

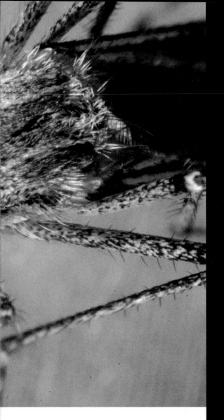

CONTENTS

Small but deadly...........

Invisible killer............

Two days of pain ....

Poison puffer ....

Zombie poison ....

Stonefish ....

Blue rings for danger ......

Piranhas ....

Killer frog ....

Poison arrows ....

Deadly snails............

Deadly spider ....

World's biggest killer.......

Need-to-know words ....

A deadly bean!/
Read more online ....

Index ....

SMALL BUT DEADLY

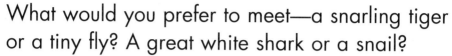

What would you prefer to meet—a snarling tiger or a tiny fly? A great white shark or a snail?

Large, fierce animals can be dangerous.

However, some of the biggest killers on Earth
are smaller than a coin!

The tsetse fly (teet-SEE fly) is found in Africa.
It lives by sucking blood from people and
animals. As it does this, it spreads a **disease**.

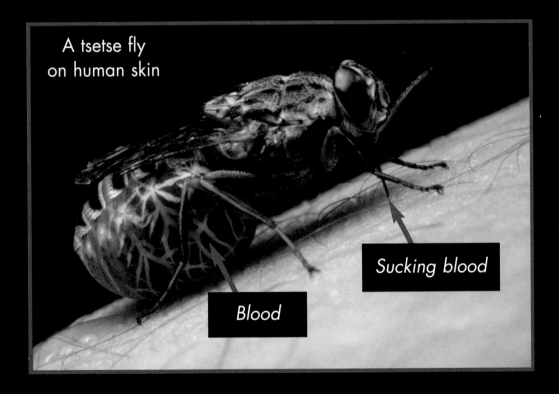

A tsetse fly
on human skin

Sucking blood

Blood

The disease, known as **sleeping sickness**, kills
thousands of people in Africa each year. The disease
makes people fall asleep—and never wake up!

The tsetse fly may be small...

...but it is **deadly**!

INVISIBLE KILLER

The most **venomous** animal on Earth is the box jellyfish. It lives in the Pacific Ocean.

The see-through box jellyfish is almost invisible.

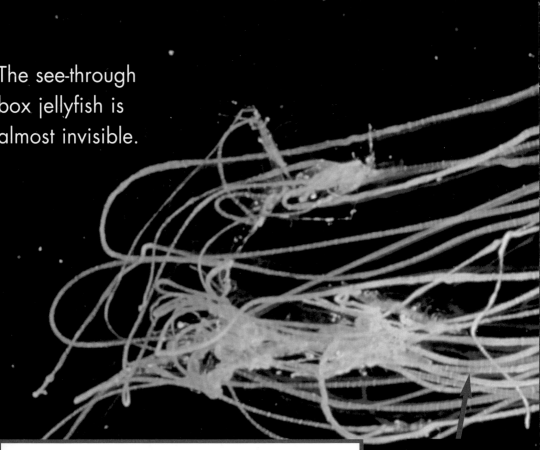

Tentacles

The jellyfish's **tentacles** have millions of dart-shaped stingers. The jellyfish fires the stingers into its **prey**. The stingers release **venom** into the prey.

A box jellyfish's sting can kill a person in less than four minutes.

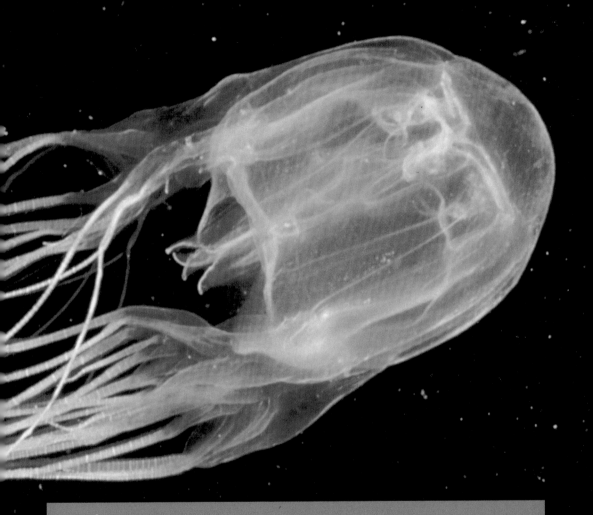

Vinegar can save your life!

VINEGAR

Vinegar can help heal the sting of the box jellyfish. Pouring vinegar over the wound stops the stingers from releasing more venom into a **victim's** body.

TWO DAYS OF PAIN

The Irukandji jellyfish lives in the sea near Australia. Its sting doesn't kill, but is very painful!

An Irukandji jellyfish digesting fish

The Irukandji Jellyfish is only the size of your thumb.

The venom causes the victim to ache, itch, sweat, and twitch. The victim feels very sick and in terrible pain.

The pain lasts for around 30 hours!

No one knows how the venom works.

A scientist was stung on purpose by an Irukandji jellyfish. He wanted to learn how the venom works. The scientist said:

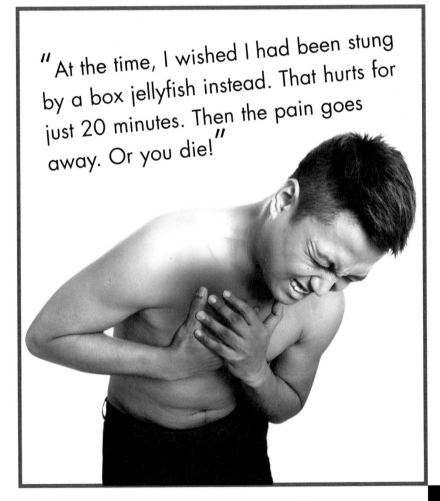

"At the time, I wished I had been stung by a box jellyfish instead. That hurts for just 20 minutes. Then the pain goes away. Or you die!"

POISON PUFFER

When in danger, pufferfish puff up into round balls. They puff themselves up by swallowing huge amounts of water or air. This makes it hard for a **predator** to bite them.

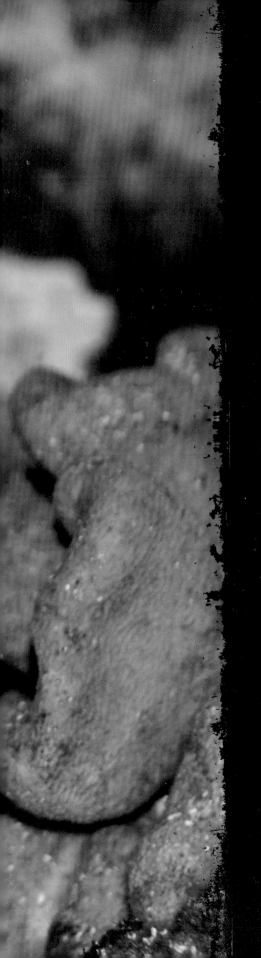

The pufferfish makes a strong, deadly **poison** inside its body.

If a person eats poisonous pufferfish flesh, it **paralyzes** his or her muscles.

In some countries, people eat pufferfish. The fish must be prepared by a trained chef so the poison is removed before the fish is served.

ZOMBIE POISON

On the Caribbean Island of Haiti, some people believe pufferfish poison is used by **sorcerers**. They believe sorcerers use the poison to turn people into zombies—the walking dead!

If a person was fed a small amount of pufferfish poison, it could paralyze him or her.

The person would not be able to move. The person's heartbeat would almost stop.

The person would seem dead—even to a doctor.

The victim might even be buried in a grave.

But then the poison would wear off.
The person might climb out of the grave.

He or she would seem to be...

...the walking dead!

STONEFISH

The stonefish is one of the most venomous fish on Earth! It lives among rocks on **coral reefs**.

If a person steps on a stonefish, the spikes on its back jab into the person's foot. The spikes contain a strong poison.

Coral reef

Stonefish

Venom squirts through the spikes and into the victim's body. The venom makes it hard for a person to breathe. The spikes also cause painful wounds.

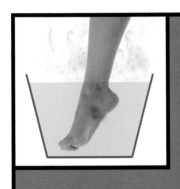

Put your foot in hot water to help the pain.

Go to a medical center right away to get treatment.

The fish looks just like a stone!

BLUE RINGS FOR DANGER

The blue-ringed octopus grows no bigger than a golf ball—but it's still deadly!

The blue rings appear when the octopus feels threatened.

The blue-ringed octopus usually stays hidden from people. It is found in shallow water and often hides under rocks. Since it is found close to shore, people may accidently step on the octopus and cause it to attack. If bitten, a person may become paralyzed. The venom may also cause a person to become blind.

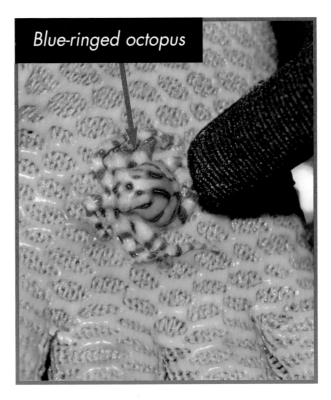

Blue-ringed octopus

The blue-ringed octopus is a popular pet in Southeast Asia. However, many owners are accidentally killed by their deadly pets.

PIRANHAS

Piranhas are little fish with big teeth.
They live in rivers in South America.

Piranhas have razor-sharp teeth.
One piranha can give a nasty bite.

But if piranhas gang together...

...they can be deadly!

Sometimes, rivers start to dry up when it is hot. When this happens, many piranhas have to live together in a small amount of water.

Then, many piranhas hunt together in a group.

When a large animal, such as a cow, comes to drink, the piranhas attack!

Cow skull

The piranhas eat all the animal's flesh, leaving just the bones.

KILLER FROG

The golden poison dart frog is just two inches (5 centimeters) long. However, some scientists think it might have enough poison inside its body to kill ten people!

The poison is in the frog's skin. Just touching the frog causes a painful rash.

If a predator bites the frog, the predator will be dead in minutes!

The golden poison dart frog lives in the **rainforests** of Colombia in South America.

POISON ARROWS

Hunters in the rainforest use poison from the golden poison dart frog on their arrow tips.

They rub the arrow tip on the frog's skin.

Any animal struck by the arrow will be paralyzed in seconds.

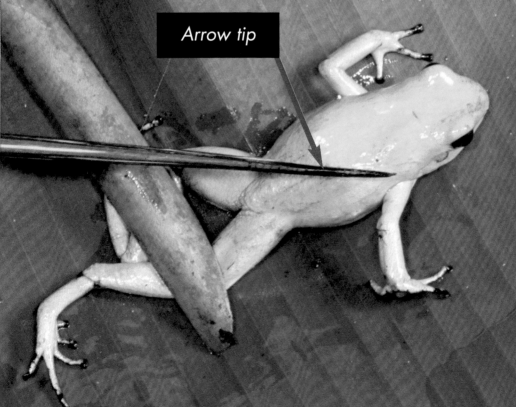

Arrow tip

DEADLY SNAILS

Dr. Jon-Paul Bingham has a dangerous job. He **milks** snails! The snails are not garden snails. These deadly snails, called cone shells, live in water.

Dr. Bingham collects venom from the cone shells. He uses the venom to create new drugs, such as painkillers.

Harpoon comes from here

Cone shells have sharp stingers called **harpoons**. Cone shells pump venom into their prey through their harpoons.

One sting from a cone shell contains enough venom to kill 15 people!

Harpoon seen through a microscope

If Dr. Bingham got stung, he would be in trouble.

Dr. Bingham told the doctors at his local hospital about his dangerous work. The doctors there know if he is stung they must get him onto a **life-support machine** fast. If the machine can keep him alive, his body will clear out the venom.

DEADLY SPIDER

The Sydney funnel-web spider is one of the world's most venomous spiders. It lives in Australia.

A scientist milks the spider for its venom. It can be used to make an **antidote**.

The spider has a deadly bite. It has sharp fangs that pump venom into its victims. Its fangs are sharp enough to pierce a human fingernail! If a person is bitten, the venom can cause nausea, sweating, and muscle **spasms**.

Hospitals have an antidote for the venom. If treated quickly, victims of the Sydney funnel-web spider will live.

Funnel-web spider in a pool filter

The spiders often fall into backyard swimming pools. They can survive underwater for up to 24 hours.

WORLD'S BIGGEST KILLER

The most dangerous animal on Earth
is the tiny mosquito.

Every year, 70 million people catch
diseases from mosquito bites.

When mosquitoes bite people, they
can spread deadly diseases such as
malaria and **yellow fever**.

Mosquitoes live by sucking
blood from people and animals.

At least one million people
die from malaria each year.

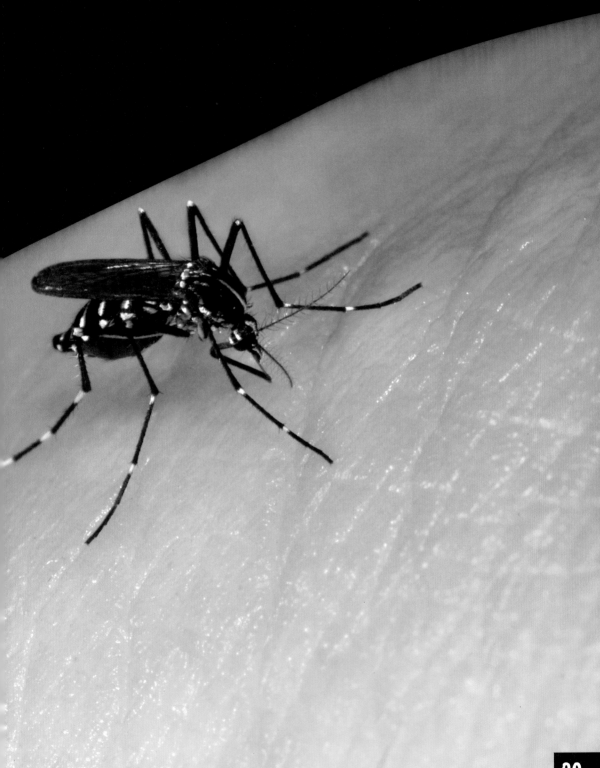

NEED-TO-KNOW WORDS

antidote A drug that stops a venom or poison from killing a person

coral reef A rocky area in warm, shallow seas. A coral reef is made of the chalky remains of huge numbers of tiny animals called coral polyps

deadly Something that causes death

disease A sickness

harpoon A type of stinger shaped like an arrow or spear

life-support machine A machine that keeps a seriously ill person alive. The machine does the work of the person's heart and lungs

malaria A disease that causes liver and brain damage. It is most common in Africa and Southeast Asia

milk To draw out or remove a liquid

paralyze Made unable to move all or part of the body

poison A substance that can kill or hurt a person or animal

predator An animal that hunts other animals for food

prey An animal that is hunted by another animal for food

rainforest A jungle of tall trees that grow in hot, wet parts of the world

ricin A deadly poison found in castor beans

sleeping sickness An often deadly disease caused by the bite of a tsetse fly

sorcerer Someone who can make magic

spasm An often painful, involuntary tightening of a muscle

tentacle A long, flexible body part used for feeling or grasping

venom A poison that is passed onto another living thing through a bite or sting

venomous An animal that uses venom to kill prey or to defend itself

victim A person or animal who is hurt or killed

yellow fever A deadly disease that causes a victim's skin to turn yellow. Yellow fever is found in South America and Africa

A DEADLY BEAN!

One of the deadliest living things is not an animal, but a bean!

The castor bean contains a deadly poison called **ricin**. If pure ricin gets into a person's blood, it can cause death. A pellet of ricin the size of a pinhead could kill a person in hours.

Castor bean plant pods with beans growing inside

READ MORE ONLINE

http://magma.nationalgeographic.com/ngexplorer/0603/games/game_intro.html

http://kids.nationalgeographic.com/Animals/CreatureFeature/Poison-dart-frog

http://www.barrierreefaustralia.com/the-great-barrier-reef/blueringedoctopus.htm

INDEX

A
Africa 5
antidotes 26–27
arrows 22–23
Australia 8, 27

B
Bingham, Dr. Jon-Paul 24–25
bites 17, 27, 28
blue-ringed octopus 16–17
box jellyfish 6–7, 9
breathing problems 15

C
castor beans 31
Colombia 20
cone shells 24–25
coral reefs 14

G
golden poison dart frogs
     20–21, 22–23

H
Haiti 12
harpoons 24–25

I
Irukandji jellyfish 8–9

M
malaria 28–29
mosquitoes 28–29

P
Pacific Ocean 6
paralysis 11, 13, 17, 23
piranhas 18–19
poison 11, 12–13, 20, 22
pufferfish 10–11, 12–13

R
rainforests 20, 22
ricin 31

S
sorcerers 12
South America 18
stingers 6–7
stonefish 14-15
Sydney funnel-web spiders
     26–27

T
tentacles 6
tsetse flies 5

V
venom 6, 9, 15, 17,
     24–25, 26–27
vinegar 7

Y
yellow fever 28

Z
zombies 12–13

Printed in the U.S.A. - BG